AN ALPHABET OF

AUNTS

AN ALPHABET OF
AUNTS

C.M.DAWNAY

and

MUNGO McCOSH

JONATHAN CAPE

LONDON

Published by Jonathan Cape 2007

2 4 6 8 10 9 7 5 3 1

First published in Great Britain in 2007 by
Jonathan Cape

Random House, 20 Vauxhall Bridge Road,
London SW1V 2SA

Addresses for companies within The Random House Group Limited can be found at:
www.randomhouse.co.uk/offices.htm

The Random House Group Limited Reg. No. 954009
www.randomhouse.co.uk

A CIP catalogue record for this book is available from the British Library

ISBN 9780224081160

Back flap portrait of C.M. Dawnay by Charlotte Millicent Dawnay

Composed and proofed by Mungo McCosh from Founder's type
and printed blocks at Robert Smail's Printing Works Innerleithen, Peeblesshire,
in the care of the National Trust for Scotland

Printed and bound in China by C&C Offset Printing Co., Ltd

FOR HUGO

IN MEMORY OF ALICE

AN ALPHABET OF
AUNTS

AMLA

B

U

N

T

CROISSANT

DISINFECTANT

elegant

Fondant

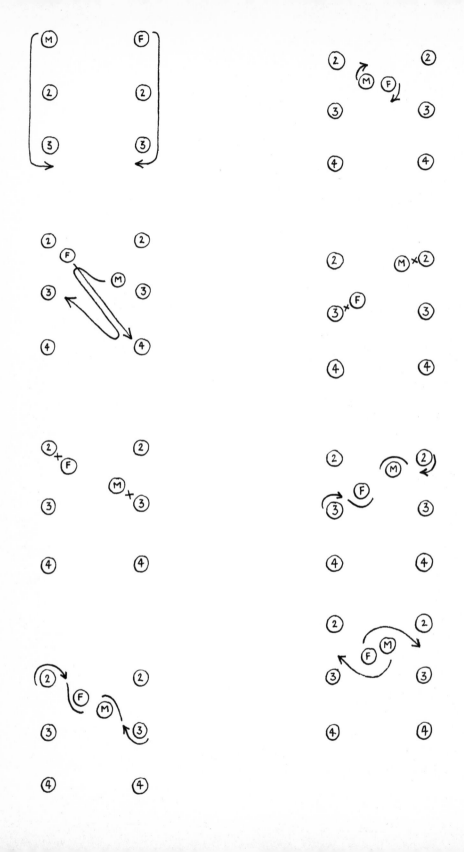

Gallivant

HYDRANT

INDIGNANT

JUBI

LANT

Kant

lubricant

MENDICANT

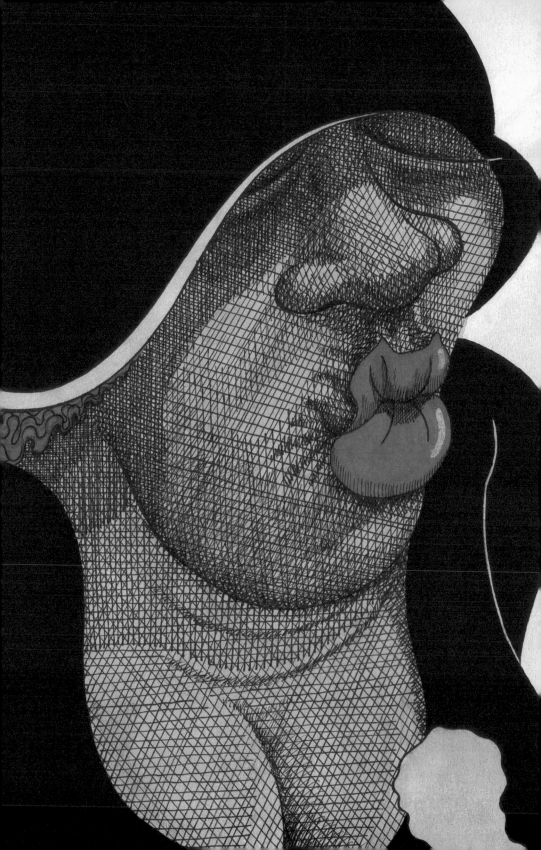

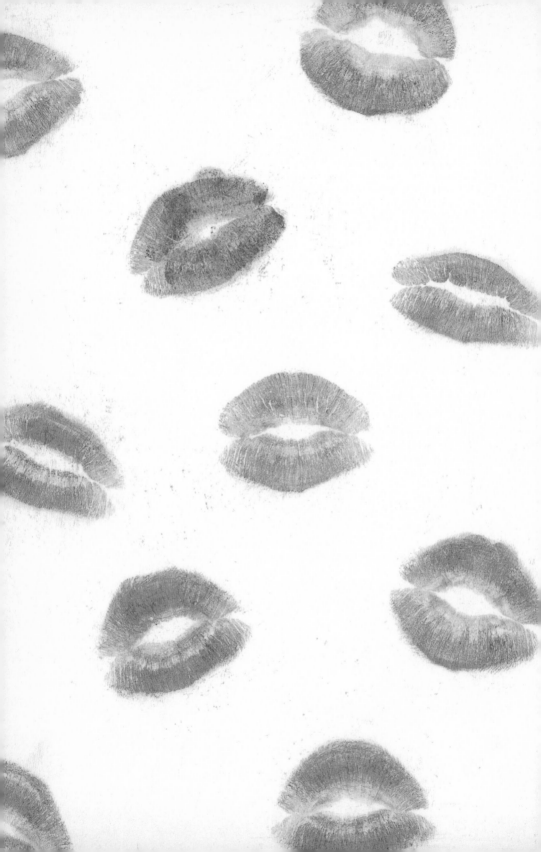

Osculant

PROTE

QUANT

Sycophant

SEMPER ABSUM

Truant (·.

undul

ant

Valiant

what

do

more

you

ECTORANT EX

E**X**AMINANT E

UBERANT E**X**F

.ARANT EXUL

E**X**ORBITANT

NT E**X**TANT E

XTRAVAGANT

AUSTANT E**X**H

T E**X**CITANT E

OHANT EVI

EXTANT

HX3 TNAT2U
AUSTANT EXH

EXTRAVAGANT
XTRVVAGANT

NT EX TANT E

EXORBITANT
ORBITANT

ARANT EXUL

IBERANT EXP

EXAMINANT I

CTORANT EX

IANI EXSICC

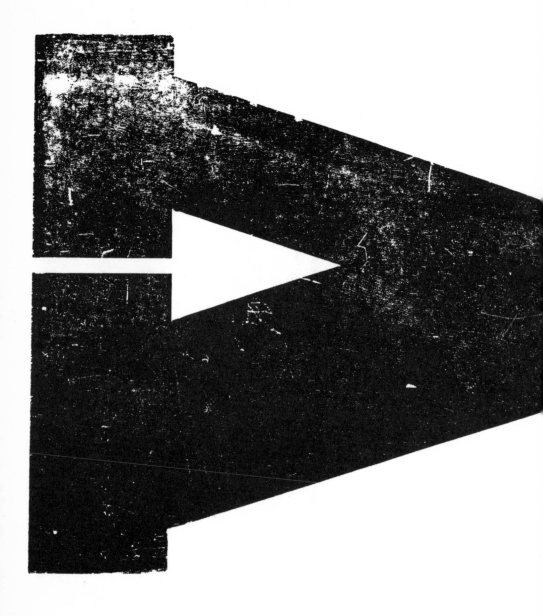

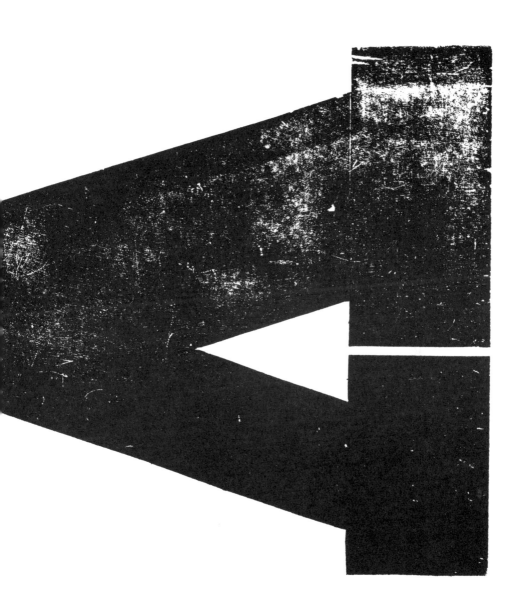

WHY

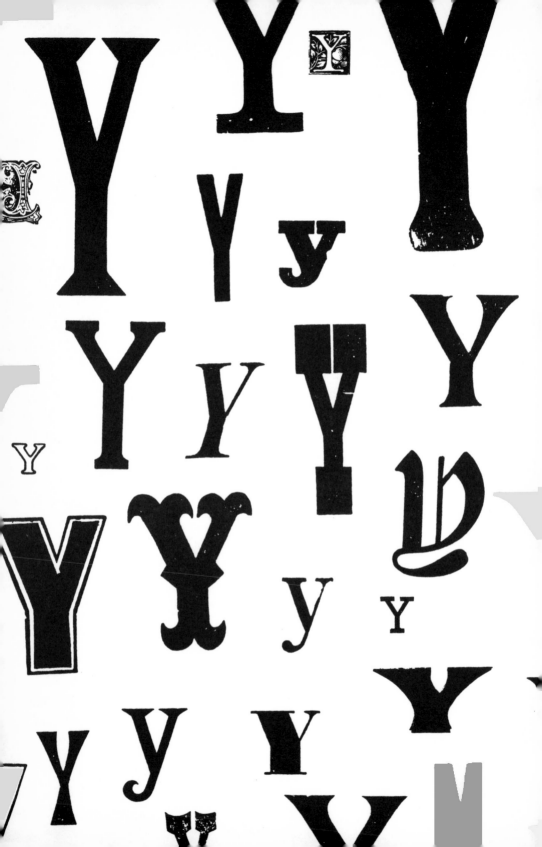

TYPEFACES

A	5 LINE PICA COLUMBUS
B	42PT PALACE SCRIPT
C	36PT GRANBY INCLINED
D	36PT PERPETUA CAPS
E	5½PT TRAJAN EXTENDED
F	10 LINE DEVINE
G	48PT RONDO MEDIUM
H	UNIDENTIFIED FLORAL INITIALS
I	8 LINE SANS SERIF CONDENSED N°.14
J	8 LINE SANS SERIF (TWO COLOUR)
K	48PT TUDOR BLACK
L	66PT GRANBY BOLD LOWER CASE
M	48PT ANTIQUE N°.3
N	12PT SPARTAN BOLD CONDENSED SIZE 1
O	30PT HEAVY SCRIPT SERIES 322
P	16 LINE LATIN ELONGATED
Q	48PT SANS SERIF N°.3
R	UNIDENTIFIED FLORAL INITIALS
S	24PT AMAZONE
T	2 LINE NONPAREIL STENOGRAPH
U	8 LINE ARTISTS GROTESQUE
V	2 LINE ENGLISH GROTESQUE
W	10 LINE OLD STYLE ROMAN
X	60 LINE UNIDENTIFIED EGYPTIAN
Y	12 LINE LATIN / GRECIAN N°.2
Z	36PT / 24PT ROCKWELL